NATURE'S BEST
DISPLAY
AND CAMOUFLAGE

TOM JACKSON

HOW ANIMALS'
APPEARANCES HELP
THEM HUNT, MATE
AND SURVIVE

{CONTENTS}

POISON DART FROG.............................. 4

MUSKOX.. 6

BLUE MORPHO.................................... 7

CHAMELEON...... 8

THORNY DEVIL................................. 10

LEAFY SEADRAGON........................... 11

RHINOCEROS.................................... 12

PANGOLIN 14

POTOO 15

PEACOCK 16

MOOSE 18

LIONFISH 20

PORCUPINE 21

DUCK-BILLED PLATYPUS 22

BALD UAKARI 24

STRIPED SKUNK 25

RATTLESNAKE 26

FRILLED LIZARD 28

BIRD OF PARADISE 29

GLOSSARY....................................... 30

FURTHER INFORMATION.................... 31

INDEX.. 32

EVOLUTION

Evolution is the process by which living things can change gradually. Over millions of years, many tiny changes add up to some big differences. Evolution is why there are so many different species living on Earth. Some species are obviously more closely related than others. In 1859, Charles Darwin said that related species had evolved from the same ancestor in the past. He explained how evolution could do that with a process called natural selection.

Animals in a species may look the same, but they all have a unique set of variations. These differences make some animals 'fitter' than others. The fitter ones are better at surviving in wild conditions than others. Darwin said that nature 'selects' these fit animals; they have many children, while the unfit ones die off. Over time, the characteristics that make an animal fit become more common, and eventually every member of the species has it – the species has evolved a tiny bit.

Thanks to natural selection, animals have evolved some amazing ways of surviving and ensuring they reproduce. The way the animal looks is very important for this. Some species

Like their namesake, giraffe-necked weevils have a very long neck. This helps the insect reach a long way as it rolls a leaf into a nest for its eggs. The males, like this one, have much longer necks than the females, which they use in fights over mates.

have evolved camouflage, so they can stay out of sight. Others do the opposite. They want to get noticed so they can impress mates and have as many young as possible. Other ways animals look come from the defence systems they have evolved. Of course, some animals have evolved to use all of these techniques. Let's explore some of nature's best and most amazing physical characteristics!

3

Poison dart frogs come out to feed during the day. They have no need to hide. In fact, they advertise their presence with brightly coloured skin. This makes it easier for predators to recognise them — and stay away. A poison dart frog's skin is full of poisons, so if a creature were to eat one they would get a very upset stomach — and could even die.

MUSKOX

The muskox lives in the icy tundra of the Arctic, where the temperature drops to -25°C in winter. To keep warm, the muskoxen grow a fur coat almost 1m long, made up of the longest hairs in the animal kingdom!

Muskoxen live in one of the most inhospitable habitats on Earth. In the short summer, plants grow very fast and herds of muskoxen graze throughout the long days. When winter returns, the ground freezes solid, and the herds must dig out tufts of grass from under the snow. In midwinter, the Sun does not come up for weeks. The muskoxen huddle in a triangular formation to stay warm. The wide end of the triangle is made by the largest animals, who stand headfirst into the wind. The younger muskoxen shelter behind them.

Every part of the muskox is covered in thick fur, including a long beard and thick socks of hair that protect the legs.

FACTS AND FIGURES

Scientific name....... Ovibos moschatus

Location.................................... Arctic

Habitat................................... Tundras

Size................................... 1.5-2.6m

Food...................... Grass, moss, roots

Life span.............................. 14 years

Young........ 1 or 2 calves born each year

EVOLUTION SOLUTION

A muskox may look like a wild cow, but it is actually the world's largest species of goat. This makes it a good example of a rule of evolution that says that animals that live in colder places (where food is often scarce) tend to be larger than their relatives in warmer habitats (where there is plenty of food all year). The main reason for the size rule is that a large body works more efficiently than a small one, and so can survive for longer without eating.

Muskoxen are named after the strong smell, or musk, that males produce in the breeding season.

BLUE MORPHO

EVOLUTION SOLUTION

These butterflies are both a master of disguise to stay hidden and an expert show-off. They are named after the shimmering blue of their upper wings, which is produced by a trick of the light.

When a blue morph is perched with its wings folded together, it is difficult to spot. The underside of the wings are mostly brown and white, and blend in with the forest. However, the butterflies need to see each other to find mates, so the males flutter through sunny openings between the trees, revealing the blue colour of their upper wings. This dazzling colour is produced by the Sun reflecting off the complex structure of their wings.

Male blue morphos are more colourful than the females. It is quite common for the males of a species to look very different from the females, and this because natural selection has worked differently on each sex. Evolution selects the fittest animals, but the characteristics that make a male animals fit are not always the same as the ones that make a female fit. As a result, they evolve to look and behave in different ways.

The blue morpho's upper wings shine even more brightly when viewed in ultraviolet light – and butterflies can see this kind of light, which is invisible to us.

FACTS AND FIGURES

Scientific name	Morpho species
Location	South America
Habitat	Rainforests
Size	7.5cm
Food	Caterpillars: leaves; Adults: fruit juice, sap
Life span	120 days
Young	Eggs laid on leaves

As the blue morpho flies, the blue colour flashes in an out of view and can be seen easily among the green leaves.

CHAMELEON

These lizards are famous for changing the colour of their skins. However, they do not do it to stay hidden. Instead, they use their colourful skin to communicate with other chameleons.

Most chameleons are green or brown most of the time. This helps them to blend in with the leaves of their forest homes. Often, people think that the chameleon can match the patterns of its background to create a camouflaged disguise. This is not true, but when these lizards meet each other in the wild, they will

Chameleons walk very slowly through the branches, scanning the leaves for insects to eat.

A tiny type of chameleon from Madagascar is 3cm from snout to tail tip, making it the smallest reptile in the world. A baby one could stand on an apple seed!

FACTS AND FIGURES

Scientific name.. Chamaeleonidae family
Location......................... Asia, Africa and Southern Europe
Habitat...Forests
Size................................... 1.5–60cm
Food.................................... Insects
Life span.................................. 3–5 years
Young.................. Eggs buried in ground

change their skin colour into a much brighter pattern. The pattern could be a warning to a rival to stay out of the chameleon's territory, or it might be a way of attracting a mate. The colour does not change in a flash, but gradually switches over a minute or so. Recent research has shown how this works. The chameleon's skin is a mixture of yellow, red and black. It also has tiny clear crystals in its skin cells. The lizard rearranges these crystals to change the way light is reflected from the skin and that allows it to blend the three different colours in the skin into the amazing patterns we see.

Thanks to their excellent eyesight, chameleons rarely miss the target when they catch prey with their long, sticky tongue.

EVOLUTION SOLUTION

Many lizards can change colour, although they are limited to being paler in bright sunlight and darker in the shade. Pale skin reflects heat better than dark skin, and so being pale during the day stops the lizard getting too hot, and being dark allows it to absorb more heat. The crystals used by chameleons to create their skin patterns are also useful for reflecting heat from the sun on hot days. It is likely that this feature evolved first and the colour changing ability then evolved from that.

Chameleons can swivel their eyes independently and so look at two things at once.

THORNY DEVIL

This spiky little lizard lives in a habitat where there is almost no running water. While its spikes work to protect it from attack, they are also the way the lizard collects the water it needs to stay alive.

When attacked, the thorny devil inflates its body with air to make it bigger and even more prickly.

Thorny devils have a soft lump on their neck. It is a decoy head. When it is attacked, the lizard tucks its real head between its front legs, so predators bite this lump instead.

EVOLUTION SOLUTION

Thorny devils live on ants. This means the lizards also needs a source of water. No one knows if the thorny camouflage evolved before the water-gathering system or the other way around. However, the unrelated horned lizards from the deserts of America also eat ants and collect water on their skin. Evolution provided the same solution in two different places!

FACTS AND FIGURES

Scientific name.............. Moloch horridus
Location........................... Australia
Habitat............................. Deserts
Size...................................7-11cm
Food.................................. Ants
Life span........................ 20 years
Young............ 4-10 eggs laid in burrow

Thorny devils are coloured to match the red-yellow sand that covers the Australian deserts. It tries to stay hidden, and if spotted by a predator it will freeze or stand and sway slowly so it looks like a withered leaf or sprouting thorny plants. The hard spikes make it tough to swallow if it is caught, but they also give the lizard's body a very large surface area, which helps to collect dew. The desert air contains moisture and at night this condenses as droplets on the lizard's body. The droplets moves along tiny grooves that cover the lizard's body and all arrive at its mouth. This means the lizard gets all the water it needs without having to find anything to drink.

LEAFY SEADRAGON

The fish's fins are on the neck and tail. They are transparent so they do not show up in the water, hiding the fact that this is a fish and not a plant.

This relative of the seahorse is very difficult to spot. The long tube-shaped body is hidden by many leaf-like extensions that make the body appear to be a tangle of seaweed drifting in the water.

The seadragon uses the chemicals in its food to change its colour, so it can blend in with the plants surrounding it.

FACTS AND FIGURES

Scientific name........ Phycodurus eques
Location.......................... Australian coast
Habitat............................... Shallow seas
Size... 30–50cm
Food..................... Shrimps and baby fish
Life span.................................... 10 years
Young .... 250 eggs brooded by male

EVOLUTION SOLUTION

Seadragons, seahorses and other pipefish have sacrificed the ability to swim well for good camouflage. They have evolved long, slender bodies that look like seaweed stalks and seagrasses. This means they have lost most of their fins. Their bodies are covered in bony plates, which make them stiff like a plant and also help provide protection from attack – but make it almost impossible to swim.

The seadragon is an example of a pipefish, which are named after the shape of their long mouths. Its jaw bones are fused into a pipe that is used to suck in tiny shrimps and plankton. The fish floats among the seaweed in shallow water and sucks in any food it comes across. The seadragon is not a good swimmer, and uses just two small fins to push itself slowly through the water. This slow progress creates the illusion that the fish is just a piece of seaweed floating by.

11

RHINOCEROS

Indian rhinos only have one horn. Some suggest these animals were the inspiration for the mythical unicorn.

The rhinoceros is arguably the most armed and armoured creature in the animal world. It has a huge bulk that can flatten attackers, a thick, armoured skin and a fearsome set of weapons on its face.

The rhinoceros is famed for its horns — it is even named after them. The term 'rhino' means 'nose' and 'ceros' stands for 'horn'. There are several species of rhino living in Asia and Africa. Most of them have two horns on their snouts. Asian rhinos are mostly forest animals and so their horns are quite small to avoid getting tangled in the undergrowth. The African species live mostly in grasslands and are much bigger all round, with the main horn reaching 1.5m in length.

The horns of goats and antelopes are made of bone covered in keratin, the same smooth material in hair and fingernails. However, a rhino's horn is made of solid keratin — in effect, it is a huge bundle of hairs locked together, which makes it incredibly strong.

The rhino's horn is mostly used for show. Rhino rivals size each other up by their horns

FLAT MOUTH
The white rhino is not named after its colour. Instead, the term comes from the Dutch word for 'wide'. White rhinos have wide, flat mouths, while black rhinos have more pointed lips.

and the one with the shorter horn usually gives in to its opponent without any actual fighting. If a fight does start, the rhino's 5-cm thick skin protects it from serious injury. The horn is also

Rhinos are very rare because they are hunted for their incredible horns. All rhino species are in danger of extinction.

A rhino is not born with horns. The horns take three or four years to grow, and adult rhinos keep the main horn sharp by rubbing the tip against a tree.

FACTS AND FIGURES

Scientific name............ Rhinocerotidae
Location........................... Africa and Asia
Habitat.............. Grasslands and forests
Size... 2.4–4.6m
Food............................ Leaves and grass
Life span................................... 40 years
Young....... 1 calf born every four years

EVOLUTION SOLUTION

The rhinoceros is a plant eater. Some species eat grass, while most eat leaves. This kind of food is not very nutritious, and the rhino needs to eat a lot of it to survive. Being large helps, because a large body is more efficient than a small one. However, being large makes an animal heavy and slow, so this is why the rhino evolved into a tough, armoured animal instead of a fast, agile one.

used to attack threatening predators. The 2000-kg rhino charges at full speed at the threat — and that is usually enough to scare away most attackers. However, rhino's have very bad eyesight and often charge by mistake. They have even been seen headbutting termite mounds and trees!

PANGOLIN

This strange creature might look like a chubby lizard, but it is actually a type of mammal. It has a few hairs here and there, but most of the pangolin's body is covered by hard plates of armour.

Pangolins are armour-plated anteaters that live in trees or in burrows dug into the ground with their long claws. Those claws are also used for ripping apart ants nests and termite mounds, and the pangolin then licks up the insects with its long, sticky tongue. The tongue is too long to fit in its mouth. Instead, it is rooted in the back of the throat, and can be as long as the rest of the body put together! However, the most obvious feature of the pangolin is its protective plates. Each plate is made of keratin, which is the same hard material that covers horns and is used to make claws, fingernails and hair.

EVOLUTION SOLUTION

The pangolin's scales provide protection from bites and stings. They are made of keratin. The first animals to use keratin were reptiles, as it made their scales waterproof. Bird feathers and mammal hair evolved from the keratin-rich skin of different reptiles. Pangolins evolved from hairy ancestors, but their hairs evolved back into scale-like plates that look like a dinosaur's skin.

FACTS AND FIGURES

Scientific name.............................. Manis
Location............................ Africa and Asia
Habitat.............. Savannahs and forests
Size... 30-100cm
Food............................. Ants and termites
Life span................................... 20 years
Young................... 1 baby born each year

The pangolin does not have teeth. Instead, it has a spiky stomach lining that crushes up its food.

The name pangolin comes from the Malay word for 'rolling up'. Many pangolins will roll into an armoured ball if attacked, exposing the sharp points of their horny plates.

POTOO

Can you see a bird in this picture? This is the potoo. By night, it swoops through the dark forest catching insects. During the day it disguises itself as a tree stump.

Potoos have a very big head, with a large mouth and huge eyes. The eyes can spot flying insects in the dark, gobbling them up mid-flight with its big mouth. The large wings (and long tail) allow the potoo to twist and turn through the trees. The bird almost never touches the ground, and cannot walk very well at all. As dawn approaches, all these body features are hidden away as the bird perches on a branch or dead tree. The wings and tails are folded against the wood, and the big, flat head helps the potoo look like a stump.

The potoo completes its disguise by closing its eyes – almost. They are kept slightly open to watch out for danger.

FACTS AND FIGURES

Scientific name.........................Nyctibius
Location....... Central and South America
Habitat.................................... Forests
Size.................................. 20–60cm
Food................................. Insects
Life span.......Unknown (about 10 years)
Young................... One egg laid on branch

EVOLUTION SOLUTION

Most birds do the opposite of a potoo. They sleep hidden away at night and feed during the day. It is likely that 60 million years ago, before most mammal groups had evolved, there were more nocturnal bird species. Since then, mammals have wiped out many of these night birds. However, the potoo's tree stump disguise is so effective that they have stayed safe from the hunters.

PEACOCK

The peafowl is one of the biggest show-offs in the animal kingdom! The male, or peacock, spreads out its enormous tail feathers to show off iridescent blue-green eye spots. A tail this long — about 150cm — makes flying very difficult for the peacock. However, it is worth the trouble, as it helps a male find a mate. The females, or peahens, will select mates with the largest, most symmetrical and shiniest tails.

MOOSE

The moose is the largest species of deer alive today, and the bulls grow the largest antlers. The antlers are used for fighting, but they are also a visual guide to how old and how strong an animal is.

Moose live in the cold forests that circle the Arctic regions. In winter, the moose shelter from the cold in the deep forest, nibbling on bark, twigs and pine needles. In summer, they wander far and wide and often wallow in lakes and rivers, eating the water plants.

Only a bull moose will grow antlers. However, these are just a temporary feature. They begin to grow at the end of the winter and are fully formed in time for the autumn

A young bull has only small antlers. Like all bulls, it also has a dewlap, or flap of skin, on the chin, which is not seen in the cows.

breeding season, or rut. During this time, bulls bellow loudly for the attention of cows, and fight off other males during antler-jousting competitions. As winter hits, the used antlers fall off, and the process starts all over again.

A mature bull's antlers are almost 2m wide and weigh 30kg.

FACTS AND FIGURES

Scientific name...................... Alces alces
Location.......... North America, northern Europe and Asia
Habitat.. Forests
Size.. 2.4–3.2m
Food........................ Leaves, bark, lichen
Life span...................................... Unknown
Young........ One calf born every summer

Every time the antlers regrow, they have more spikes, or tines, than the year before. After about 10 years the antlers have become wide, flat panels with tines all around. Females and rival males alike can see how old a bull is by the number of tines. They also look to see how symmetrical the antlers are. As a bull reaches old age the antlers become more wonky and misshapen. Rival males will size up their antlers. The one with the smaller, less handsome antlers generally backs down without a fight.

DEER DANGER

The moose is the most dangerous animal in North America. They do not attack people but frequently injure drivers when hit by cars in road accidents.

EVOLUTION SOLUTION

Having large antlers makes it harder for a bull moose to move through the forest and escape an attack from predators, such as wolves. So why did they evolve? The huge antlers are the result of a type of evolution called sexual selection. Females choose mates with big antlers. Their male offspring therefore have big antlers, and their female ones chose mates with big antlers, and so the same thing happens in the next generation. As a result, antlers evolve to be bigger and bigger.

Antlers have a bone core covered in soft, folded skin, known as velvet. When the antlers are fully grown, the bull will rub the skin off against a tree to expose the hardened bone inside.

Moose antlers grow 1cm a day during summer. The male moose devotes a quarter of its energy to making new antlers.

LIONFISH

The stripes are a warning sign that this fish will sting.

This fish goes by many names. It is a turkey fish for its feathery spines, a zebrafish for its stripes and a firefish for the pain of its sting. Whatever you call it — don't touch it!

The lionfish lives around coral reefs, where it hunts for smaller fish. It uses its large fins to block their escape and corners them, before swallowing them whole. Other fish, even those it does not eat, know to give this predator plenty of room. Although they are not used when hunting prey, many of the sharp spines that grow out of its back are venomous. When threatened, the fish will swim with its head down so the venemous spines point towards the attacker.

Lionfish venom is not fatal to humans, but a sting is very painful. Putting the wound in hot water will destroy the venom and ease the pain.

FACTS AND FIGURES

Scientific name............ Pterois species
Location......... Indian and Pacific oceans
Habitat................................ Coral reefs
Size................................... 5-45cm
Food.......... Fish, molluscs, crustaceans
Life span............................ 15 years
Young......... Bags of eggs laid on seabed

EVOLUTION SOLUTION

The lionfish belongs to a larger group of stinging fish called the scorpionfish. Their venom glands evolved from mucus glands that all saltwater fish have. This mucus is like the gooey slime that comes out of our noses, and sea fish use it to cover their skin. Salty water draws water out of a fish's body making them dehydrated, and the mucus is a barrier to stops that happening. The mucus is also a protective layer stopping parasites from reaching the skin.

PORCUPINE

This large rodent wants to be left alone. It shuffles around at night looking for plant foods and hunkers down in a den during the day. If a creature tries to grab it, they will get a nasty jab from the porcupine's many spiked quills.

Porcupines live all over Africa and southern Asia, but the North American species is the largest type in the world. It is a slow-moving forager that uses its sense of smell to find food. If any predator looks like it might attack, the porcupine turns its back and waggles its bristled tail. If the predator pounces, it will get some of the porcupine's long quills — which are actually stiff hairs — stuck in its skin. The quills have

a barbed tip, which makes them very hard to pull out. More often the tip stays in the skin after the quill snaps off, and this creates a long-lasting sore.

FACTS AND FIGURES

Scientific name..... Erethizon dorsatum
Location.......North America, Africa, Asia
Habitat.............. Forests and woodlands
Size.. 60-90cm
Food...... Twigs, roots, leaves and fruits
Life span...................................... 6 years
Young...... 1 or 2 young born in summer

The porcupine climbs trees to reach fruits and fresh leaves, and often falls out because it cannot see where it is going!

EVOLUTION SOLUTION

The American porcupine is not very closely related to the species from Asia and Africa. All use long, spiked hairs as a defensive weapon but this is an example of convergent evolution, where unrelated animals evolve the same body features to help them survive in similar habitats around the world.

DUCK-BILLED PLATYPUS

Few animals looks as unusual as a duck-billed platypus. When European naturalists first saw a specimen of one, they thought it was an elaborate joke. However, the platypus's mismatched body parts all have a role to play.

The name 'platypus' means 'wide feet', and refers to the animal's webbed feet, which it uses for swimming along the bottom of lakes and rivers. The animal also waves its flat tail up and down to power through the water. Down in the gloomy water, the platypus needs to find food hiding on the riverbed, and this is where the duckbill comes in. This is an electricity detector, and it can pick up the tiny electric fields produced by a prey's body, even when it is buried in the mud.

Even though the platypus has a furry body, like all mammals, it does not give birth to its babies. Instead, it lays eggs like a bird or reptile. However, like other mammals, when the baby platypuses hatch, their mother feeds them milk. But there is another difference.

Platypus venom causes a lot of pain, but it is not fatal to humans. However, it is powerful enough to kill a small dog.

Duck-billed platypuses have defensive spikes, or spurs on their back legs. The males' spur also injects venom, which is used to stun rivals during the breeding season.

FACTS AND FIGURES

Scientific name..Ornithorhynchus anatinus
Location............................... Australia
Habitat........................Ponds and rivers
Size.................................. 40–60cm
Food.................................. Shellfish
Life span........................... 10 years
Young........................... Eggs laid in nest

Instead of producing milk through a teat, the liquid comes out of holes in the skin, and the babies lick the drips off their mother's fur!

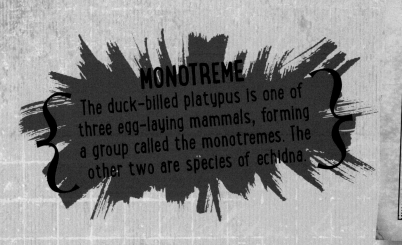

MONOTREME

The duck-billed platypus is one of three egg-laying mammals, forming a group called the monotremes. The other two are species of echidna.

EVOLUTION SOLUTION

The duck-billed platypus is related to the earliest mammals, which also laid eggs. The mammals that evolved to give birth to young were much fitter, and natural selection wiped out the egg-layers. But the platypus has survived. The reason is its electrical detector duck-bill. As far as we know, no other mammal has evolved this ability.

A platypus can dive under water for ten minutes at a time.

BALD UAKARI

This Amazonian monkey looks like it has lost all of its hair. However, the bald head and bright red face are actually a sign that it is very healthy.

The bald uakari lives in an area of the Amazon rainforest that is flooded by deep water for months at a time. It collects fruits and leaves in the treetops during the floods and climbs down to the ground to gather seeds when the waters recede. Mosquitos lay their eggs in floodwater, and the monkeys are frequently bitten by these bloodsuckers. Mosquito bites spread diseases,

Bald uakaris exist in four subspecies. They all have red faces but their shaggy fur coats range from pale yellow and white to red-brown.

such as malaria. A monkey is severely weakened malaria but can survive for several years. However, the disease will make its face pale. Therefore, when uakaris select mates, they look for the healthiest monkeys with the brightest red faces.

Amazonian people call the uakari the English monkey, because it looks like a sunburnt tourist.

EVOLUTION SOLUTION

Evolution is happening even when a species does not appear to be changing. A species is always under attack by parasites, like the microbe that causes malaria. The parasites are evolving to be better at attacking a host, and so the host must evolve to defend against these attacks. Biologists call this the Red Queen Effect. This refers to the queen in the Alice in Wonderland stories, who runs but never gets anywhere.

FACTS AND FIGURES

Scientific name.............. Cacajao calvus
Location........................... South America
Habitat..................... Flooded rainforests
Size................................... 40-45cm
Food............. Fruits, leaves and insects
Life span............................ 12 years
Young.................1 infant born each year

STRIPED SKUNK

The striped skunk is a nocturnal animal, and much of its fur is black to make it hard to see in the dark. However, it also has two large white stripes that run from the head down to the tail. If you look where they are pointing you will get a nasty surprise!

The skunk's white stripes are meant to be easy to see, day or night. They are a clear warning to larger animals to leave it alone. If a predator has never seen a skunk before, it may decide to attack. However, it will only do so once. The skunk tries to shoo away the attacker by growling and raising its bushy tail to reveal a white underside. It also arches its back to look larger and stamps its feet. If this fails, the skunk twists into a U-shape so its head and rear-end are facing the attacker. Then, it sprays a fine mist of liquid out of its anus all over the attacker. The spray's bad odour is so strong it can be smelled two kilometres away! The attacker flees and will leave skunks alone in future.

EVOLUTION SOLUTION

The skunk's smelly spray is produced by glands that have evolved from oil glands, which all mammals have. These glands are used to apply waterproofing oils to the hair and skin. Other animals use these kinds of scent glands to produce an identifying smell, used to tell who is in an area.

Skunks prey on snakes because they are immune to the venom of many American species.

The striped skunk is most active in the twilight of dawn and dusk, when it uses its sense of smell to seek out all kinds of foods.

FACTS AND FIGURES

Scientific name........ Mephitis mephitis
Location............................ North America
Habitat.................. Woodlands and fields
Size.. 35-45cm
Food.................... Worms, snails, insects
Life span.. 6 years
Young.......... 4-7 young born each year

RATTLESNAKE

The rattlesnakes are among the most poisonous snakes in the Americas. They use their venom to kill rats and other small animals, but it is also a defensive weapon. However, before a snake bites an attacker, it gives a very clear warning.

EVOLUTION SOLUTION

Rattlesnakes are not born with a rattle. Instead, the rattle grows as the snake sheds its skin. A reptile's skin is covered in waterproof scales, and these need to be replaced as the animal gets larger. Many snakes, including rattlers, moult their entire skin all at once. (In other reptiles the skin falls away in chunks.) The snake's rattle evolved from a mutation that meant a small scrap of skin was left on the tail after each moult. Instead of being a problem, this mistake became a useful way of saving valuable venom.

IMITATORS
Many non-venomous snakes wiggle their tails in an attempt to fool attackers into thinking they are rattlers.

The rattlesnake's head is a wide arrow shape thanks to the large venom glands on either side.

The rattlesnake's alarm is a soft, buzzing rattle that is supplied by a series of hard buttons of skin on the tail. The rattle is the snake's first line of defence and as it sounds that alarm, it prepares the second line: most of the snake's body forms into a neat coil, with the rattling tail tip held up in full view. The coil forms a solid foundation for the front third of the body, which rises up in a flat S-shape with the head facing the attacker. If the snake choses to bite, it will straighten this raised section, so its head lunges forward with lightning speed. Only the most nimble of attackers can get out of the way in time.

But the snake does not want to bite if it does not need to. The venom is of more use for killing prey, and often a defensive bite from a rattlesnake is dry. In other words, very little

The rattle is made from hardened buttons of skin. A new button is left behind every time the snake sheds its skin.

venom is pumped into the victim through the fangs, and the attacker is relatively unharmed. However, that attacker will know to avoid any snake that rattles out the same kind of warning in future.

Experts are finding that desert rattlesnakes are evolving a more powerful venom as their rodent prey become immune to the poisons.

FACTS AND FIGURES

Scientific name.......... Crotalus species
Location......... North and South America
Habitat......... Deserts, prairies, forests
Size... 50-150cm
Foo............................ Lizards and rodents
Life span.. 20 years
Young....... Up to 21 young born at once

FRILLED LIZARD

At first glance, this large lizard looks like any other. However, if it feels under threat, the lizard will put on one of the most startling displays in the animal kingdom.

The frilled lizard spends most of its time up trees, searching for insects and other foods. However, it does sunbathe out in the open sometimes. It stays motionless to avoid detection by predators, but if it does come under attack, the lizard opens its mouth wide to reveal its bright pink gums. As it does so, a wide umbrella of skin spreads out sideways. This makes the big lizard appear to be more of a giant.

The predator is startled by this display, and the lizard wastes no time. It turns around and runs at top speed on its back legs to the nearest tree – and safety.

EVOLUTION SOLUTION

The lizard's neck frill did not evolve to startle attackers. Instead, it was first used (and still is) to regulate the animal's temperature. On cold days, the lizard opens up the frill to catch more of the warm sunlight. The frill can also be used as a radiator to lose unwanted heat.

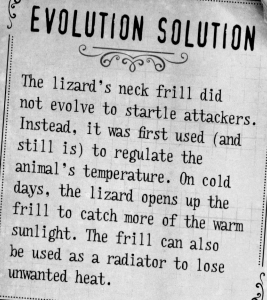

The lizard gives a menacing hiss to add to the effect of its startling frill.

The frilled lizard lays its eggs underground. The babies already have the frill when they hatch.

FACTS AND FIGURES

Scientific name	Chlamydosaurus king
Location	Australia and New Guinea
Habitat	Dry forests
Size	85cm
Food	Insects
Life span	10 years
Young	6-10 eggs laid in sand nest

BIRD OF PARADISE

Male birds of paradise have some of the most elaborate feathers of any bird. The plumage is put on display in a beauty contest as the males try to win a mate.

When the first specimens of these birds were bought back to Europe by explorers, everyone who saw them marvelled at the amazing feathers. However, the birds' legs had been removed to preserve the animals for the journey. Everyone assumed these beautiful birds flew all the time, and never touched the ground – like an angel. As a result these species became known as birds of paradise. Of course the live birds do perch, including when the vibrantly coloured males gather to attract mates. The males perform displays over and over to show

There are 41 species of bird of paradise.

The greater bird of paradise is one of the largest species. Males display close together to get the best audience.

off their plumage, and females choose a mate with the brightest colours and most symmetrical feathers.

FACTS AND FIGURES

Scientific name... Paradisaeidae species
Location........ New Guinea and Australia
Habitat.................................. Rainforests
Size.. 35-45cm
Food.. Fruit
Life span..................................... 30 years
Young......... 1 or 2 eggs laid every year

EVOLUTION SOLUTION

Natural selection works by the fittest individuals having more offspring than the weaker ones. In many cases – including birds – it is the female that choses the mate. All the male can do is attract her attention. As a result, the male birds of paradise have evolved very elaborate ways of showing how strong they are.

GLOSSARY

Arctic The region around the North Pole. The Arctic is always very cold and frequently frozen over.

convergent evolution The independent evolution of similar characteristics in different species.

evolution The process by which animals, plants and other life forms change gradually to adapt to changes in their environment.

extinction When all members of a species have died out so that particular kind of life form disappears.

female The sex that produces eggs and gives birth to babies.

habitat The kind of environment that an animal lives in. Each species has evolved to survive in its particular habitat.

hunted To be pursued and killed.

male The sex that produces sperm and, in almost all cases, does not give birth.

mammal A type of animal that grows hairs on its body and feeds its young milk.

mucus A slimy liquid used by animals to keep body parts moist or create a protective layer.

naturalist An expert in natural history.

natural selection The process by which evolution works. Natural selection allows individuals that are good at surviving to increase in number, while those that are less able to compete go down in number.

nutritious Containing a lot of chemicals that are useful for the body.

nocturnal To be active at night.

predator An animal that hunts and kills other animals for food.

prey An animal that is hunted and killed by a predator.

reptile An animal that has scaly skin.

sexual selection Natural selection through the preference by one sex for certain characteristics in the other, when choosing a mate.

solution Something that solves a problem.

species A group of animals that share many characteristics. The main common feature is that members of a species can breed with each other. Members of different species cannot produce young successfully.

territory An area that is controlled by an animal or group of animals. The territory is where they find food and build their homes.

venom A poison produced by an animal that is pumped into its victims, either by a bite or a sting.

FURTHER INFORMATION

BOOKS

THE WORLD IN INFOGRAPHICS: Animal Kingdom,
by Jon Richards and Ed Simkins (Wayland, 2014)

SUPER NATURAL ANIMALS,
by Leon Gray (Wayland, 2014)

WHAT IS EVOLUTION?,
by Louise Spilsbury (Wayland, 2015)

WEBSITES

www.zsl.org/kids-zsl

The kids' section of the Zoological Society of London's website is packed with animal information, games and activities, as well as the latest scientific studies.

www.natgeokids.com/uk/

Animal-related facts, pictures and games from the kids' section of the National Geographic website.

www.bbc.co.uk/nature/adaptations/Camouflage

The BBC Nature website has several videos about animals and camouflage.

INDEX

Africa 8, 12, 13, 14, 21
ant 10, 14
anteater 14
antelope 12
Arctic 6, 18
Asia 8, 12, 13, 14, 18, 21
Australia 10, 11, 22, 28, 29

bald uakari 24
bird 14, 15, 22, 29
bird of paradise 29
blue morpho 7
butterfly 7

Central America 15
chameleon 8–9
convergent evolution 21
coral reef 20

deer 18
desert 10, 27
duck-billed platypus 22–23

evolution 3, 6, 7, 10, 19, 21, 24
Europe 8, 18, 29

field 25
fish 11, 20
forest 8, 12, 13, 14, 15, 18, 19, 21, 27, 28
frilled lizard 28

goat 6, 12
grassland 12, 13

hunted 13

lake 18, 22
leafy seadragon 11
lionfish 20
lizard 8, 9, 10, 14, 27, 28

mammal 14, 15, 22, 23, 25
moose 18–19
muskox 6

natural selection 3, 7, 23, 29
New Guinea 28, 29
North America 18, 19, 21, 25

ocean 20
offspring 19, 29

pangolin 14
peacock 16
peafowl 16
poison 5, 26, 27
poison dart frog 4–5
pond 22
porcupine 21
potoo 15
prairie 27

rainforest 7, 24, 29
rattlesnake 26–27
reptile 8, 14, 22, 26
rhinoceros 12–13
river 18, 22

rodent 21, 27

savannah 14
sea 11, 20
sexual selection 19
shellfish 22
shrimp 11
snail 25
South America 7, 15, 24, 27
species 3, 6, 7, 12, 13, 15, 18, 21, 23, 24, 25, 29
striped skunk 25

thorny devil 10
tundra 6

variation 3
venom 20, 22, 25, 26, 27

woodland 21, 25
worm 25

Published in paperback in 2018 by Wayland

Editor: Julia Adams
Designer: Rocket Design

Dewey number: 591.4'72-dc23
ISBN 978 1 5263 0762 0
Printed in China

10 9 8 7 6 5 4 3 2 1

Picture acknowledgements: Cover: © Shutterstock; p. 1, p. 28: © Dave Watts/naturepl.com; p. 3 © Nick Garbutt/naturepl.com; pp. 4–5: © Michael D Kern/naturepl.com; p. 6: © Orsolya Haarberg/naturepl.com; p. 7: © Stephen Dalton/naturepl.com; p. 8: © Nick Garbutt/naturepl.com; p. 9: © Stephen Dalton/naturepl.com; p. 10: © Jouan & Rius/naturepl.com; p. 11: © Alex Mustard/naturepl.com; p. 12: © Jean-Pierre Zwaenepoel/naturepl.com; p. 13: © Uri Golman/naturepl.com; p. 14, p. 31: © Pete Oxford/naturepl.com; p. 15: © Juan Carlos Munoz/naturepl.com; pp. 16–17: © Paul D Stewart/naturepl.com; p. 18 (top): © Andy Trowbridge/naturepl.com; p. 18 (bottom): © Eric Baccega/naturepl.com; p. 19: © Jose Schell/naturepl.com; p. 20: © Georgette Douwma/naturepl.com; p. 21: © Patricio Robles Gil/naturepl.com; p. 22: © Roland Seitre/naturepl.com; p. 23: © Dave Watts/naturepl.com; p. 24: © Ingo Arndt/naturepl.com; p. 25: © Rolf Nussbaumer/naturepl.com; p. 26: © Daniel Heuclin/naturepl.com; p. 27: © Edwin Giesbers/naturepl.com; p. 29: © Tim Laman/National Geographic Creative/naturepl.com; p. 30: © ; all images used as graphic elements: Shutterstock.

The website addresses (URLs) included in this book were valid at the time of going to press. However, it is possible that contents or addresses may change following the publication of this book. No responsibility for any such changes can be accepted by either the author or the Publisher.

Every attempt has been made to clear copyright. Should there be any inadvertent omission, please apply to the publisher for rectification.

Wayland, an imprint of Hachette Children's Group
Part of Hodder & Stoughton
Carmelite House
50 Victoria Embankment
London
EC4Y 0DZ

An Hachette UK Company
www.hachette.co.uk
www.hachettechildrens.co.uk

MIX
Paper from
responsible sources
FSC® C104740